About trying to understand his parents, Tim Seibles says, "It's like watching them through thick glass," but the distortions of magnification and detailed focus that mark these poems that are at once a homage to family, as they are a confrontation with the complex feelings that surround the fact of aging, represent an opportunity for Seibles to write some of his most affecting clear-sighted poems to date. These are profoundly vulnerable poems that are distinguished by the risk and daring that we expect from our best poets. Those of us who have come to enjoy Seibles' lively language code-switching, his alertness to the political and social realities of our time, his alluring sensuality, and his splendid and welcoming humor will be wholly satisfied by this beautiful collection; but his careful charting of a poet's life beginning with the accident of his birth, the elusive story of his parents' histories, as seen from this present personal and historical moment, make this one of his more important collections to date. Seibles is an essential American poet, and he wears this mantle with sheer mastery, endearing self-deprecation and grace in *One Turn Around the Sun*.

Kwame Dawes, *City of Bones: A Testament*

Through precise language, striking and intimate images, a paradox of smart irony and disarming sincerity, and a persistent awareness of the pressure of economic and political realities, Seibles offers us a rich and memorable inquiry into a life. When I turned the last page of *One Turn Around the Sun*, I felt like I'd just finished a wonderful novel.

Ellen Bass, *Like a Beggar*

Tim Seibles. When the world grows nostalgic, he swings real. When the world turns bitter, he stretches out his arms in verse. When the world tries to deny, he stares it in the face and tells the truth. Then asks it for a dance. I'm tempted to say *One Turn Around the Sun* is Tim Seibles' best book, but that'd be like saying Beethoven stopped at eight symphonies.

Cornelius Eady, *Hardheaded Weather*

ONE TURN AROUND THE SUN

Also by Tim Seibles

Fast Animal

Buffalo Head Solos

Hammerlock

Kerosene (chapbook)

Ten Miles An Hour (chapbook)

Hurdy-Gurdy

Body Moves

ONE TURN
AROUND THE SUN

TIM SEIBLES

etruscan press

Etruscan Press
Wilkes University
84 West South Street
Wilkes-Barre, PA 18766
(570) 408-4546

www.etruscanpress.org

Published 2017 by Etruscan Press
Printed in the United States of America
Cover painting: Bili Bidjocka
Grâces & Intentions & Grâces, Smithsonian National
    Museum of African Art
Image courtesy of the artist
Photograph by Franko Khoury, 2015, Smithsonian National
    Museum of African Art
Cover design by L. Elizabeth Powers
Interior design and typesetting by Susan Leonard
The text of this book is set in Adobe Jenson.

First Edition

16 17 18 19 5 4 3 2 1

Library of Congress Cataloguing-in-Publication Data

Names: Seibles, Tim, author.
Title: One turn around the sun / Tim Seibles.
Description: First edition. | Wilkes-Barre, PA : Etruscan Press, 2017.
Identifiers: LCCN 2016004680 | ISBN 9780990322184
Classification: LCC PS3569.E475 A6 2017 | DDC 811/.54--dc23
LC record available at http://lccn.loc.gov/2016004680

Please turn to the back of this book for a list of the sustaining funders of Etruscan Press.

This book is printed on recycled, acid-free paper.

For my parents:

     Thomas Sumner Seibles III and Barbara Lutticia Bluford
     without whose love I would not exist.

     And in memory of Jack Myers: poet of the awakened
     heart, mentor, pool shark, and friend.

     With special thanks to Natalie Fish for her unwavering
     interest and encouragement.

Now the world is buried in me, to the hilt.

--Jenny George from "Sword Swallower"

ACKNOWLEDGMENTS

I would like to thank the following magazines and literary journals in whose pages many of these poems first appeared.

Amistad
Beloit Poetry Journal
Blue Lyra Review
HEArt Journal
Massachusetts Review
Poetry
Shenandoah
Split This Rock
Terminus

Anthologies

Bearden's Odyssey
Double Kiss
Of Poetry and Protest
Uncommon Core

ONE TURN AROUND THE SUN

CHAPTER 1

ODE TO YOUR MOTHER

Do you remember yourself
six months after conception?
Far from the egg, your heart
chirping like a hungry chick,
those unwalked feet—fat crickets
kicking around, eyes blind
as buttons: cell by cell,
rod by cone, getting ready
to call up the colors and lights

and your mother, often craving
licorice with apple pie, outside
catching a bus with you—
in her warm pond—a golden koi
nosing the surface for bits of bread,
you: the unnamed stranger
coming for the long stay,
traveling all night, your face
taking shape in the shadows

or maybe   she sees herself:

a bass drum with something
booming inside her, a small theater
off-Broadway with someone soon
to be famous pacing the wings—
so much promise! Were you restless
to begin?—all your vitals rehearsing
their hard parts. Did you have any sense
that she was out there?—your brain

almost building itself   a secret
mansion— a million doors
to a million rooms, each
with a candle, your little head
holding the Milky Way
rekindled in miniature: consciousness,
The Great Mischief, waking up

to try again—one particular
flicker in the cosmic sea, a starfish
riding the big back of a blue whale—
which swims like a planet   gliding
the sun's slow waves with you

beginning to insist
inside this woman you hardly
know, though she is Everything,
steadying her new weight
on Earth. Your heart

blind as a kite—wind
on the rise, three months
from *Day*. Did you suppose
an inkling   of what would be
out there— the invisible air
filling us up, rabbits in hats,
hints, houses, banana slugs,
bacteria, and trees!
Other people—

the look
on your face   already amazed

or whatever comes
just before that.

ODE TO YOUR FATHER

So Sunday nights
he put on Yusef Lateef
and that flute stole secrets
usually locked in the moon's
cool house   and you watched
his head nod yes to all
he couldn't say, then tiptoed
back to TV, hoping he'd forget
it was past your time for bed.

When he yelled at you,
you probably heard
his father yelling at him,
though you couldn't
recognize the flat "don't
talk back" settled beneath
his voice like a big bass
at the bottom of a lake.

Growing up, he said *yes sir*
to that brassy baritone and
wasn't his father's father's voice
a part of him too, that part
that seemed tied up
in some long ago trouble,
even when he sat in the shade
baiting a hook.

Hard to picture it now: him,
in his straw hat and high water
dungarees, Oklahoma boy
moping home with a loaf of bread,
his buddies teasing and tempting him
back to the park. How did he

face his first bully?—the one
that cracked his tooth
and cut his arm. Ever wonder
where he got that
hot-grease-in-the-face glare?—
the look that made you
so afraid: his father
made him fight that
tough kid twice—

and at times, didn't the whole country
try to break his skin?—waiting for him
on every corner like a bully. What
did he make of all those stores
that wouldn't let him in? He worked
the slaughter house—stiff
with dry blood, his overalls
could stand by themselves.

In spite of this, you found him
years later: your pop mopping the kitchen,
whistling "My Satin Doll," a tune
you hadn't heard, so half-listened
as if he were some odd station
on the radio. And when he'd start

the old "things were different
back then," it sounded like *once
upon a time*. You shrugged
and secretly rolled your eyes,
but half of you is still made
of him: his long arms, his love
of hats, your solitary heart: half
jazz, half ready to fight.

Your father didn't kiss you
like your mother did, but
every October he drove you
to the arboretum to see
the blood-orange leaves, even
when he had a lot on his mind.
That mind

you'll never see inside,
though you know it's packed
with good songs, some hard feelings,
and all the stuff he will not say.

COMPOSITE

Your weight

on one foot, then
the other,

walking—
that taste of baked
bread so bright
your mouth is born
again. December:

a coin,
cold circle
in your hand—
each

of us   made
from two people:

your body,
an angel's

tambourine—
the self, something

like lamplight

on a slush-covered
street: can

someone else

see what I mean?
Does everybody

hear that slight
ringing

THE HILT

First Session

Have I been here
before? Will this

happen again.
Alone in bed or not:

the unlit room
taking and refusing

shape. Some questions.

Some numbers on the clock.

Sometimes I sleep   and then
this dream: behind a fence

some faces
bandaged, some

people insane: some

stare at me   others talk

Who else is there

with you?

Late. A moon that fits
    between two telephone wires
        stalls over the streets. Philadelphia:
            Upsal and Boyer, the corner

                where my life began. Small
                    shoes—I remember: small
                        coats and small galoshes
                            in winter.

In the store window, I see myself like someone else: people walk their coffee, tethering their thoughts: each life an itchy scarf. I think   I am *not* them. A voice in my head assures me—over and over.

But you see the same thing in their eyes, that same hesitation: the way a child looks into a busy room

Once upon a time   my mother's gingerbread
and her big laugh. And before his stroke, my father
next to his Oldsmobile—a photograph: he's waving,
right hand a little higher than his head. It looks like
he almost smiled.

In her mind, my mother
still lives with
her parents, though they
died before I was
ten. She'll say she
saw them
at breakfast. She's
as sure of this
"as the day is long."

She'd swear
"on every bible
in the world."

Your first
kiss, whose

porch
was that?—

two o'clock sun,
tiptoeing up
the steps—

and now, Vanessa's
gone: can you

prove her soft mouth, her
twelve-year-old fingers

lighting the hair on your wrist?
You say   her blouse

was sleeveless—you think
her skin   was midnight brown

So   all the days have added up to this: when I look into a mirror, I
see
a mirror looking back at a mirror.

   The wise one said, "The sugar   cannot taste itself."

Maybe this is what it means   to be singular, to be a sound without
an
echo   to be a little afraid all the time.

Does your
skin

make noise
no

matter how
you try

to keep it
quiet?

I've seen the look that means

insane—the look that says: *there's a party*
inside my head   but they won't

let me in

       Eyes, open windows, rain
all over the mind.

       Alone—like walking
on the moon, like one fly

standing on a sandwich.
              You—holding
your phone   like someone's

really in there

For a few seconds, I had my hand on the chest of the man I was guarding—
basketball, accidental, but still his heart knocked against my palm.

The door to a life   that thin. Today there's rain, a gray wind, and
wherever you are, warm blood revolves from a nudge beneath your ribs:

mostly, we don't notice, but we look around all the time   and when light
is bad, we squint.

.

What do people see
when they see you?

My mother has dinner and
minutes later asks "when do we eat?" When I
mention her husband upstairs she laughs,
"never got married, not me."

I say who I am   and she says,
"I'll have to look into that."

So, even memory   turns its back
and, bit by bit, like dim things

in a darkening place, the details
hide themselves

somewhere inside us, though
once we knew our lives

were lit by them.

When I ask myself

about myself   and all of you
around me, there's only

this *talking*—

I can barely hear
anything else

CHAPTER 2

GENESIS

It starts
sub-atomically: one quark
rubs a neutrino
a little bit
wrong, one particle

of light cuts the dark
just by being
itself. Then
as if from nowhere,
protons><electrons:

atoms begin
to stake out turf.
Without supervision, they
slouch into cells, flex
their walls,

becoming whatever
they want: paramecia, amoebas,
viruses—each
always a little hungry

for something
else. Of course,
they get around
haphazardly,
at first—carried

by wind or water;
then someone
requisitions
a single slippery foot,
soft, much too slow—
but soon

the invincible
exoskeleton: hard body
built for taking
over. One

after another
the numbers grow
underground

until

cities emerge: short
mounds rising
from dirt,

and they come—

alert antennae,
polished heads,
jaws like teeth—

single file,
riding six legs

NO COMPLAINTS BLUES VILLANELLE

All this stuff happened before I got here
Cars clog the highways; our taxes build tanks
I'm not complaining, just can't see it clear

I look in the mirror and the face seems sincere
Turn to the future, but it seems to have shrank
I'm not complaining, just can't see it clear

Just one of those days that happens every year
I ain't in the news—hard not to give thanks
Alotta shit happened before I got here

You walk into church and try not to sneer
Just want a prayer you can take to the bank
You're not complaining. God knows it ain't clear

Who's to say that I couldn't be queer?
When you fill out the forms, do *you* fit in the blanks?
I'm not complaining; I wish it was clear

You'll catch me chillin' at the bar with a beer
What's not to like when the Right closes ranks?
They got it all wrong before I got here

When you go to the movies, the monsters are clear,
But back in the world they run all the banks
Alotta stuff happened before we got here

Sometimes this shit   gets a little severe
Can't blame the folks who use dope to get tranked

Who set this in motion before we got here?
It's just a question—just wish it was clear

EIGHT BALL

My father   was not amazing
at pool. Sighting along the stick,
he would stare down the cue
as if some stout, albino animal
had paused on the green.
Then he'd shoot

and scatter the others, the lucky ones
disappearing. I probably beat him
as much as he beat me—all the welts
from his parenting quietly
driving my shots. Sometimes,
when he was "feelin' it," he'd hit

a banker, the 5-ball bending
back soft into the side pocket,
and the pride on his face
shimmered like summer heat
rising from asphalt.
It was usually

early evening: my mother
in the kitchen with Walter
Cronkite chalking up the news
on CBS, as though his
solemn delivery could set up
some better headlines.

At the time, of course, I just
wanted to win. Didn't think
about what those whuppins
meant   or why he used that
old ironing cord, but I did
crave a little revenge, hoped

to even the score somehow,
especially when my late teens
found muscles rallying
under my skin. I really thought

I could go toe-to-toe with him:
get in some good shots—
show him   what it meant
to be overpowered and afraid.
I had gotten a lot taller
by then—and probably
might've taken him down.

Some days he'd say *shut-up!*

And I felt like a young god
done wrong by this dumb Dad—
his thick moustache, his good
gray slacks—who said he knew me
"like the back of his hand,"
and my veins were racked
with adrenalin ready to help me
break the whole damn house.

But my pop   was often a shy man
who wouldn't raise his voice
to my mom. He joined the church
chess club and stayed out
of bars. Sometimes I'd see him

alone in the living room   brass
blasting from the stereo, a Marlboro
cooking in his hand—and though he never
said so, I think he would have loved
making music, saying loud with a sax
what he could never fit into words.

One time   he hit me

and I nearly fell into that
glass table by the hi-fi,
but he caught me, left me

tracing the shock
of his knuckles
that, for a few days,
defined the left side
of my face. It couldn't

have been easy   coming home full
of fury, the only black biochemist
at a government lab, shaking hands
with all the extra shit he had to take.

If my son   had mouthed off
I like to believe I wouldn't
have blacked his eye.

I don't have any children

and no hide-away
pool table that folds out
from the back of a couch,
so it's hard to get a clear shot
at what might be true
with so many rough maybes
sitting in the way. Still,
I bet my father's life was a lot

harder than mine   and I'm
pretty sure he believed
all he did   was mostly
exactly what he had to do.

MORNING WHERE YOU ARE

"Don't go around looking like I would if I could
but if I can how can I" -- Mom

Some spring days
she and her sister, Eva,
strolled up Boyer Street,
and you could tell

they were The Bluford Girls
again—blue suits, black heels,
gold pins—and early April
pulled up in its cool limousine.

I was a teenager then
and had no idea what
that walk meant: the royalty
in it, the defiance—how

in what seemed a few years,

what could never end
would end: my aunt dies
on a bad mattress,
one flat soda in the fridge,

and my mother, stolen
from herself, her smile
no longer made
for her mouth.

———————

Maybe now   it's always sunlight
splintered behind the trees: evening,
the wind down. Cars,

like conversations, pause
and move on—my mind walking
its three-legged dog

from this   to that
and once more, I begin
to think about Barbara Bluford,

English teacher, pinochle player
born on a train bound for Virginia:

my mother grew up a city girl,
proud of her father, the one
black dental surgeon in Philadelphia.

When I was little, I'd sit on her lap
and wave from the window: *my* father
waving back, headed for the bus.

It was the early 60s: the news
just beginning to bleed.

She was kind and solid in that
take-no-nonsense parental way
and dressed so sharp

that a glimpse might cut'cha.
Those hats she wore to church:
bronze feathers blazing against gold

or the rose crown with the cream band
braided around a brim so wide
it held another sky.

*

Some nights we played *Pokeno*.
Four glasses, grape Kool-Aid:

me, my brother, and my Dad.
She filleted the cards
like a 5-star chef.

The kitchen clock adding up,
the tiny jackpot ripening.

*

My mother swears she's never cooked
a turkey, though for five decades,
she did it twice a year. Last Wednesday,
she started pouring *Wheaties*
at sunset. I was on the phone,
"It's evening, ma—*evening.*"
She said, "It may not be morning

where *you* are, but it's
morning here."

Before the bad dentures,
she had the gladdest smile—

a morning unto itself:
any day starting over
wherever she found us.

"In college,"
my father said,
"she used to smile
like that   at *me.*"

———————

When she slipped in the lecture hall
he picked her up— Fisk University,
September 1945:

WWII barely over, fall-out still flying the stratosphere.
Lamplit nights, my father below her window,
his Kappas to her Deltas—the brothers in chorus,
his hopeful solo climbing the ivy   *Only you…*

*

Picture the lit major
in Arna Bontemps' English class: her mid-calf skirt,
her blouse, blue jay blue, the matching pumps,
hand up, the answer a lantern in her eyes

and Mr. Chemistry, Thomas Seibles, III—
dapper cat from OK City, snap-brim hat,
pin-stripe suit, spit-shined shoes, that easy
side-to-side shuttle of his shoulders when he walked:

*

my nearly adult parents, beautiful—
their bodies still brand new.
On their honeymoon, Niagara Falls
must've flashed over them like an avalanche,

a passion like sunrise that first time,
like meeting a Prophet and having all
the answers asked.

———

Growing up, I thought
I knew what   was what,
the hammer of each day

barely missing me, me
with my mother's face,
my father's heavy hands,

so this is what
what　turns into—bits
of your life straggling
behind you—empty cans
hitched to the newlyweds' car

or the ragged tail of one red kite,
my father playing it
like a big fish in the sky,

and my mother
brushing my *Brillo* head,
teaching me the wonderful
"cinnamon toast" and how
to act in church

and not to wear polka-dots
with plaids.

COMPOSITE

This breeze
soft as a child's arm.

Over there, steam from a coffee
walking off.

You go somewhere,
then somewhere else: your life.

When did you open your eyes?

It's as if I'd been asleep
and woke up

to Mrs. Hopkins and the ABCs!

Somebody teasing, my straw
leaning in a small carton of milk,

finger-paints, *Pop Goes The Weasel!*

So many days circling
the musical chairs.

If the self
is a small ship

one of its sails,
some of the time,

grows plump
with air like this

WALK

Dusk in the body,
    starlight near the heart.

One half-lit street
    heading into night: now

the insects magnify
    their small vocabularies

as if talking   to you
    your shadow sharp,

almost alive
    beneath the lamp.

_____

Do we live to scuff each
    hour   dragging the hours

past?— as if you could
    see best by turning back—

the Present   with Her lips
    soft on your neck / the future

filling with ghosts.

I still remember
    the first dog I ever saw:

that crazy tongue, the one sound
    flashing between its teeth.

Days when *Crackerjacks*
    crashed their music in me,

and crabgrass sizzled
    with chiggers, us playing tackle

till the sun ran out of breath.

_____

Where was it
    that your heart first

opened? Where, when you first
    began to shutter its rooms?

Your mind gradually bending
    beneath the suspicion

that life   would not
    save us, that *love* itself

was little more than a hook
    for the mouth—time spent dying

quietly, driving to work.

_____

Car radio: the yammer,
    that itchy fuss, each bit

a ballpeen hammer
    chipped against your skull,

and the street somehow
    miles away, the funhouse

distance   between your *self*
    and everyone else. To be awake

means what? Hearing

that voice start over
    in your head, the worries

walking in place: the argument
     backlit—*why do you*

do this? Thinking,
     thinking: your brain caught

in the swarm. Words
     telling you what not to say.

————————————

I have tried to pass
     as an almost reasonable man,

as if that could mean much
     these days: Cruelty showing off

His sample tray of meats.
     Have enough

people died? Has first dark
     found your shadow

in a vague circle of light?—the day
     walking off, hard news

turned rot in your mouth.
     Is it true   the mirror

has confused you
     with someone else?

————————————

Maybe it is too easy
     to say *darkness* and mean

trouble or whatever it is—
     what we can't fight, what

the years do to us:

that smoldering sense
    of having been taken

prisoner, though you sit there
    almost a fly   feeding—

sunlight like sequins
    on your faceted eyes.

———————————

A woman goes by with pants
    like liquid glass   and I catch myself

leaning on memory: the promise
    of people we don't

know. I have been
    a stranger: that first hour

in someone's arms

when it seems we will
    never want again—

as if touch held
    the cure to this

chronic condition: the
    half-knowing / being half

understood: this blink
    and smile, the way we go

outdoors with the other things
    held inside our faces—

so I'm older now,

———————————

but maybe the safest thing we can do
    is insist on what might not be

found here, this hopeful walk
    toward *Neverland*. I think about

Fear, its steady governance
    all over   and what people

are willing to believe
    to keep from being alone—

the mind spurred
    to build its own cage:

hatred or the hunger
    for *God*   an ache for

money—how a
    mob becomes a

country becomes the
    history   against

which   we must break
    our lives.

———————————

What I've become: this
    running clock, this heretic, these

brushed teeth, this cock
    covered in cloth, this gang

of muscles wearing down,
    my brain a nest just starting

to burn: this *this*

that I carry around.
    Tell me,

wherever you are, tell me
    just how hungry we might be:

forks wet with food
    filling the opened faces,

all day the daylight
    eaten.

———————————

From his garage, a man
    and his hammer rattle birds

who'd been near sleep: now
    the branches chick and chatter,

now the ants reconsider
    their silence   and something else

comes clear: the veins
    in the leaves are the same

in your hands—Time starts walking
    into voice—you see yourself

on a street: three miles
    before starlight, one late wasp,

almost blind, climbs back
    to its place   in the eaves.

CHAPTER 3

THE HILT

Second Session

The see-saw, I remember—
    my big brother stranding me
        up in the air: the
            bright green willow, red
                ants running the trunk.
              Sunday school. This was

                    behind the church. Japanese
                  beetles were eating the roses.
                    I wore a fake tie clipped to my
                      stiff, white shirt

Having ushered you into the who-knows-what that waited in the world,
having seen your face before that first hard glint hacked your eyes,

when they look at you late in life, do your parents find anything familiar?

Sometimes I think
I see myself. Am I on TV?—

getting
a sandwich,
starting the car,
calling somebody,
calling back—
bizzy.

After awhile, the sun looks
over its shoulder. *Every day,*

in this window,
a mannequin
turns his
perfectly
trained
face

The self is real, right?—this who-you-are, this
soft wheel: these chronic recollections—

Does it feel like a trick?   This thing

you've become: some dream re-running
in your veins, what you   believe,

the way you walk—some sign
of a life-long shove: your mind,

a shy animal, force-fed, skinned

In the video

before the
police came,
Tamir Rice
was a kid

playing a-
lone in a
park near
the gazebo.

I used to do that.
I'd have my football with me, a water-gun in my pocket,
maybe some *Sugar Babies*.

Before the
uniform
opened
fire,

do you
think that
boy had
any idea

his story
was al-
ready
written?

Afternoons I would sit in the basement building houses with *Lego*.
Laundry hung from the pipes and when someone
opened the door, the draft made the shirts
move like ghosts.

The bones beneath my face—my mother's cheeks, my father's tough brow. How they've added up in me: my brother and I, their lengthening shadows.

Late at night, I find myself thinking like a man overboard, like someone up to his neck:

> *you find yourself*
trapped at a certain age,

try to move   try to gnaw through your leg:
whatever it takes—
> *reason against reason against everything*

So many days I'm in this coffee shop,
writing to make a case for the beauty that begins and ends
with us.

> In the parking lot, there's this guy yelling
> at everything   no one else
> can see. His
>
> pants are wrecked, his ragged afro,
> mostly gray. He does
>
> not see himself   being
> seen. He does not
> know where he has gone.

"Death hides in the world

so we disguise ourselves"

/ if we can.

Born the year of Emmett Till, as if a country could itself be a kind of

knife, I have lived with some hate   like a blade eased in and with-
drawn carefully. This is the slow way. *Your heart*

fractured like a skull   but your face seems the same, the streets look just
like streets and

look how the day burns down while you reach for a different history—
time filling the air   like sunset

Will this
happen again?—

the whole thing
a circle: us

walking around and around
touching the fence:

mean religions, dumb schools—

us   the lab animals
ruined over and over—

this senseless sweat,
these unslept nights, the self
swollen like a sprain

CHAPTER 4

TASTE ME BLUES VILLANELLE

"The Mad Hatter's tea party
is the whole fuckin world!"

--overheard

Not sure what I'm doin'   and can't say where I'll be
People think they know me but don't see how I am
When they get me, I bet the germs enjoy me

I grope along this broken road from sea to shining sea
The madness roots inside me, while I revise my plans
Looks like what I'm doin' might make me what I'll be

Isn't it enough we're stuck   and cannot fight or flee?
Weather burns the world of men; tornadoes walk the land
When they stop me, I hope the cops enjoy me

The time has come, the Walrus said to talk at many things
I turn around to look around and try to take a stand
But don' know what I'm doin' and can't say what I mean

I've always been an optimist   so that is what I'll be
I'm at your door with *Wonder Bread*, some butter and some jam
If you kiss me   I think your lips'll like me

Daylight is the splintered plank I walk into the sea
Got up with a hustle   but went down flimmed and flammed
When muthafuckas find me, they'll wonder who I be

I'm at the Hatter's Party shovin' honey in my tea
The time we saved, the wage they paid felt something like a scam
When they bite me, them greenhead flies annoy me

Won't say I'm a token, but can't say I rode free
You'll catch me at the Starbucks—broken donut in my hand

Don't like where it's goin', but that's just how I'll be
When they taste me, I hope the worms enjoy me

49

MAGNIFYING GLASS

No one
would burn
your name
for not seeing
the ant's
careful antennae
testing the air
next to your
shoe, six legs
almost rowing
it along. Who

would be upset
if you brushed one
off-handedly off
your arm, undone
by the tiny
steps: *what do
they want*,
you ask—unaware
that they breathe
through their
sides. Do they
sleep? Do they
dream
anything? No
one should

mark your soul
short   if you
mash one: when
two ants meet

there's no tongue
for hello—it's a
bug, a nearly
less than

little thing: at most,
made to chisel
crumbs
under the fridge
with eyes that,
even in brightest
day, see not reds
or greens but gray
and gray again.
Who would

curse your life
if you bring out
the *Raid?*
How many books
have they
read?—that
brain   a virtual
speck. Is all
they carry
really work
or just some
dumb old daily
ado?—the heart
spending

what blood, what
prehistoric nudge
on those
handsome,
brittle heads.

ONE TURN AROUND THE SUN

Early day, early summer, liquid sunlight
soaking the city and crape myrtle trees bring back
their pink and purple blooms: how can it happen
again, again— Earth spins and dawn unwraps
the night world as if to say *show me a story*
and the eyes blink

and hearts turn over—something like engines, maybe
like clocks—and not only in beds but in branches—
the chickadees, the quick squirrels, the katydids
and underground, the ants: the million-million hum
that one note that makes the grassroots giggle—
and what about this chronic itch, this brimming
sky that asks everything to come on:

the emerald moss, the millipedes, the old
oaks holding their ground—even shade glides
like a cool animal, while people smolder
secretly   as if *self* were a sort of fever,
our heads rising as if we might sail: Monday,
Monday,

then Monday— a month of days,
a month like a cricket   in your hand
then gone. I can't understand
Time   how it makes us and makes us
disappear. I keep turning back
to memory—my life, 59 years spent:
my job, a dead parrot on my shoulder,
bills flocking like flies to the corpse:

what can anybody do? Time
running like ants all over the afternoon
and where are *they* going with so many legs—

as if it made sense to live in a frenzy,
as if their legs had a life of their own
and the little things were getting carried away,
their pepper-speck eyes reading one version

of what daylight brings: Trouble and his
magic hat   what the night almost hides—
the homeless brotha, his missing teeth
a trail of crumbs to the Starbucks
parking lot, "Back in the day, I played guitar,"
he grins—some glint of good music
glossing his face. My shades
muffle the glare: me with my
paper money / him with his
hand open

like the door to a house
already burning   or waiting to burn, ready
to burn for both of us—the dollar bills, a book
of matches—and I see what passes for kindness
may not be kind but some kind of clumsy apology
for the monster that mouths *them that got
shall get*, The Moloch that eats every woman,

every man: some bitten in the womb, some later,
some so gently they don't even feel themselves
slip-slide into the throat   and we all try
to dance to this—the prevailing sound
mistaken for music: the humpty-hump
krunked-up bumping hiphop could be the cry
of a country going under for the third

time: *everybody put your hands in the air
and wave'em like you jus' don't care*—
cells and phones, twitters—tweets, charged
and re-charged, telling   telling each other
what? as the big teeth close around us.

When I was a boy, I would get up early
and go outside— summer coming on
like the smell of cinnamon toast—a little dude
shod in sneaks, primed in shorts, my voice
a piccolo! I remember the red ants
on first patrol   strolling up my shins
with a bold nonchalance, giving me
that cool once-over. I could hear them
muttering all they had to do before dusk—

something like discontent twitching a few
antennae: *Why am I out here with six legs and
no pants? I could live for a year on three strawberries—
fuck the colony!* Even then, my mind threw itself
toward what nobody said: my new brain
filling like a blister, the ruckus inside me,
a carnival come to town.

Early summer, Saturday   free time
soaks the city   and this slow-walking woman—
the rich potion of well-made hips, the accent
of such motion slightly muted beneath
her black shorts and, of course, I hear my blood
getting dressed: first swerve of self
towards a better orbit— heat lightning

on the heart's coast—the sexual chance,
the Great Maybe: and what about the brave
shock of first touch, the sumptuous crush
of a kiss, the groove communion—thigh
studying thigh / so much of this displaced
by jobs, by septic religion, ghost-dick capitalism,
television—the anytime friend, bright star

with make-believe light, the come-hither
and scold of this colony called America.

I look at facebook: the hopeful eyes
peeping from the cyber window, the need
to be *seen*, known; I look

at people in bars,
beer and nachos, cooked beef appearing
then gone—young men, young women:
the unconscious ooze of such
beauty   and flies landing
unnoticed, planning a future:

war, wars like hit songs   the torn skin
of the daily scrum—cars restless at red lights,
millipede pedestrians, *kill zones*, the big buildings:
boxes full of work to be done, bosses / drones—
bizzy, the word repeated

until it becomes a city itself—everyone
zigging to the zag: blue collars rub
the sore machines, executives graph the goods,
call the shoppers who catch the scent
with their long snouts.

I see the brown faces,
hard masks trying not to look
surprised   by the undeclared siege—
the Mainstream deftly sicking its dogs,
sending the guns, locking the doors,
night flaring her cloak, the moon
bitten, never whole again: I think
about children   how they

smile when we smile, how we
agree not to say what
we know, not to know
what we know   about growing up:
the calendars gone bad, weeks

dashed to chalk, children
squeezed, their big heads
scored in the vice, gnawed
to the cob

like the rest of us—and all
that's left of me now is my want
for that woman who walks a bass line
so slow even her shadow wants to *holla*.
She doesn't know how sincerely
I would praise the caramel-chocolate
sea-salt of her secret body, how well
I would forget the churches and mosques,
the synagogues, the come-along schools.

Give me the pagan cathedral
of a woman's cunt, the dawn
of her mouth meshed with mine,
the good Goddess giddy in her eyes,
the blood in harmony—what time,
what drink so smooth,
what justice better
than the justice lovers do?

Once, once and *once upon a time*,
they tell me I was born, but
I can't remember the muscular push,
the hands, the clanging light.
According to my mother, it was August
and I cried loud   and *loud*.
Wish I knew where they were,
that class of 1955, the nursery choir
that had me burbling a solo—hour
after hour, all of us blind, our little lungs
changing the air: I look back,

I look back at myself looking back,
but the fact is, one morning I was found
on Earth and strangers learned me their ways—
this noise they call speech   and how to act:
right now, I am *behaving* myself—
check out the baby goat gumming
my brow, the normal shirt, pants zipped,
the mischievous eel penned down—I keep
trying to behave: *Act like you have some sense,*
my father says / *Easier said than done,* I say.

It's all I can do to keep from pissing on tree trunks and storefronts,
marking my turf like a two-legged tomcat, scratching this life
as if I belong: I spend alotta time being polite, but
some people   *should have the shit slapped out of'em*—
and not only presidents and priests, born-agains
and racist pricks but everyday people

like me   who dress up for the status quo, buy
The Beast a burger, then get a half-hearted dry-hump
and a Frenchless kiss in return—fingering
receipts, checking my watch   when I should soak my soul
in kerosene, strike my head like a match! How many
seasons have I nixed for a job? How much craving
tazed in my trousers, while all summer

America becomes *The Land of Tiny Shorts*:

such visibility!—oh me, oh my—
as if I had never before, as if every photon
had flown to teach me light: the swarm swarming
even now: what can I do?—my life, *my life!*
eats my life—already 59 years gone

and some of my friends
gone to ground or gone gah-gah
for *God*   which is worse:
the voluntary blindness—

to chew the same verses
over and over
with the grim donkey—
as if the Earth was not
a hummingbird, as if staying
awake   wasn't scripture enough.

Woke up in my wrecked apartment—
a stack of bills, piles of books, fucked up floors,
stuffed-up nose—couldn't talk
myself out of bed: my coffled heart,
my face stained and washed again,
again until I look like a man trying
to look like a man, but I'm here— *here,*
this minute   finding myself
snared in the threads. Have you
ever seen that? A bug moving, then
the sticky tug of what had been
invisible: the mean realization—the sudden

uh-oh knowing exactly what's what:
Death   its bizzy legs   closing in
to tie you up. When I was a boy I threw ants
into webs and watched / didn't know
it was a preview of my life: *believing,*
believing what I saw, what I'd been
told to see   and everywhere

the slaughter houses wearing
their golden arches, the soldiers
declared necessary, the mantra, *pay more
and save*—the matrix, the tortured
script   disguised as fun, disguised
as your *career,* disguised as a "brand
new car," as credit, as marriage,
as the nuclear family, as Christmas,

as *a day off*, so you can catch up—
the outcome already unmistakable: this
is why the mad go mad, why
the riots and revolutions come back:

this story, this tall tale of brighter
whites and bigger blacks, them prisons
for profit, that football fantasy, this
corporate democracy, these techno
cronies— us bizzy monkeys, we
monkeys on-line, all them monkeys
on TV—this story is not

our story: to live for *that green*, to be
all about *the shiny things* is to be chummed
and gaffed—is to wake up with a barcode
for a face, to know dawn   as a soldier
sent by the clocks— a prod, a shove,
a hangman petting the scaffold.

Dawn   I knew it once:

peach light, new sky, liquid summer swimming
the breeze the way Her mouth brushes your ear.
Dawn's kiss on the thigh of my soul! My eyes—
two loons, twin musketeers, ten orgasms,
twice kings—revoking the governments and their
armies, rescinding the weekdays and the legions
dying for coffee, dying inch by inch
in the quicksand, in the *getting to work*.

Suppose, just once, you saw a middle-aged maniac
skating telephone wires like a squirrel, or one
glad woman jumping balconies and boulevards
as if time were a trampoline—think how gladly
you would lose your mind: look
what the *Takers* have taken and the monsters

they have made, the tame zombie-playmates
they have made of us: smiling, bobbing
for the job, trotting along, when we might be trolls
under their bridges—billy goats butting their
smug asses—when we might re-write the world!

What is that restlessness? What is this rage?
Proof that the rose still burns in your blood—
root and branch, thorn and bloom, proof
that your brain is a bucking horse, that even
a dog remembers and bites the leash; I want
such teeth in *my* mouth. Why can't we
have a world worthy of the wheeling sun?
The Earth is a house that flies!

Fuck all the powers that be.

I remember my parents—my mother
trilling her soprano, my serious father
and his black fists, how they kept on
despite the heavy sleet strafing
their lives: they should be famous
for getting dressed   the morning after
Martin Luther King was killed: I was thirteen,
puberty coming on like a seizure—

I went to the kitchen. My cereal sat there, sugar
snowing on the brown flakes, my mother tilting
the spoon, my father with his Cherokee eyes, cup
rising to his lips, getting ready for the day, getting
ready   no matter what, doing the *had to be done.*
I can't recall what they said, but they were calm—

my brother stabbed his eggs. There would be
riots at Germantown High—and my parents went
to work surrounded by white people who measured
their words /
                    I sit here with these pencils meaning

to make some sign, some song, something
like the love I've been given. I feel the pulse
pecking my wrists, but I don't know:

I don't know:

Early sunlight, broken summer, buttery day
the dawn brims over—crape myrtles and cars,
the city birds call to each other, all the people
simmering 98.6 degrees, this blood
shuffled with history, the DNA

whispering *persist! persist!* Everybody
a political prisoner, every one of us force-fed
some version of what the daytime brings,
what the midnight hides.   Already Death
sketches my face, my beard drawn gray.

Century after century, He opens
his scabby arms, while rise upon rise,
little kids rush the land, tasting the details,
meaning to take it all back, believing themselves
the first, the smartest, the true: *back in the day,*
I was a child and everything was a soft cookie!

But the members of the Klan were babies once
and the officers of the Third Reich too and the killers
called *Janjaweed*   and Dick Cheney and his puppet,
The Idiot, and Tojo and the Taliban,
and Assad and Mugabe and everyone
who swung a blade in Rwanda, and the
rapists running the rape camps—and the
chemists who chemmed napalm
and the Khmer Rouge, and all the slave
masters with their bizzy cocks and every
gun-gaming cop and the man who shot
Mahatma Gandhi: every one   a child once,

coming from the rainforest warmth
of a woman's womb, every one
taught the amnesia—like me:
I was the goofy boy

pressed into knickers and knee socks—
my mother tucked a napkin under my chin,
made gingerbread with black strap molasses,
read me, *The Billy Goats Gruff, Little Black
Sambo, A Child's Garden of Verses*— how I grew
beneath the sky of her voice, how ready to run:

> *Eenie-meenie-mynie-moe*
> > *Catch a doggie by the toe*
> *If he hollars let him go—*

I hid and chased, flew and fell—was wings
and no bird, my legs spinning
as if they had a life of their own.

I spend adulthood trying to blend in, trying
not to be the stranger who's become strange—
trying not to be *It*: that lost brotha
in the parking lot trying to sing,
smelling like moldy piss and dead dog
with no lovers or friends, with no place
to sleep   though sleep has become harder

and harder to find / O friends! The sun comes back
again, again—only to find us strumming our
dim teeth, filling our pants, sucking the workday's
mangy tit, while the ants, the trillion-trillion

hum just beneath us: do you think
they think   we *know* something? I've held a few,
felt the ready bite of those tiny jaws. Imagine
your own self grabbed

by something ten-thousand times your size
and deciding to bite it! To be in the clutch
of a monster and still sink your whole life
into one stupefying chomp meaning *get off me
goddammit!* Isn't that what courage is for?—
to lay claim to your life, to roam beyond the grasp,
beyond the rule of whoever means to use you as fuel

for bad machinery. Break open your eyes!
the night—without being asked, with no vote
and no compromise—backs off for the sun.
The days are more than we say they are: dawn
gives birth to them all, names none—
the minutes riot, time flames in every direction.

Let's get out of this, this

stupor called *a normal day*, this dumb farm
called *country* / We starve
with the feast nearby and swallow
the words of a story nobody wants to tell
but why? Why be practical?—when The Hour
rips Her gown, kicks down your door

and wraps Her big legs around you—why pretend
you *don't* know what I mean?
                                                    Yesterday,
after thrashing a *Tastykake Krimpet*,
I saw an ant stealing a crumb way, way
bigger than possible—I was downtown:

Chevys flexed their engines, pedestrians pushed on—
sandals, high heels, sneaks, bizness kicks—some mouths
smoking, some spending talk through a small box,
trying for the ear of someone invisible, someone
who makes the daily knock hurt less.

I believe it is hard to be human, to be these
new animals, hard to say yes to this singular
blood   and to the flying world that made us:
Who keeps conjuring the Distractions? Who?

What are the Words that gnaw on the soul?

Our heads smolder and blaze, slow light
gaining the streets—maybe now,

maybe now   it is time
to be born:

early day, open summer, a slight breeze
over the sleepers, our tired legs

on edge— we circle the sun
in so many ways: *this* Earth

and all the other planets
holding their own.

CHAPTER 5

ZOMBIE BLUES VILLANELLE

There are days I believe there is nothin' to fear
I rev up for green lights, my engine on call
But it could be the zombies are already near

That sleep that we feed every day of the year
What's up with your friends when they circle the mall?
There are nights when I think I have no one to fear

My Mom watches *Oprah*   to sweeten the year
You can keep your eyes open, see nothing at all
But it might be the zombies are already near

You think life is s'posed to be lived in this gear?
Been askin' that question till my brain has gone raw
Certain days I believed I had nothing to fear

I have dreams where I'm drivin' with no way to steer
You can growl like a cello; you can chat like a doll
At the games, ain't it always the zombies who cheer?

I think *fear itself*   is a whole lot to fear
I have watched CNN till it made my skin crawl
I might be a zombie that's already here

I been pounding this door but don' nobody hear
You can drink till you think that you're seven feet tall
Fast dances, good chances, and nothin' to fear

You can fly through your days until time is a smear
Maybe blaze up the bong   or blog out a blog

There'll be days when you know you've got nothing to fear
But you could be a zombie   that's already here.

AT 59

after Randall Jarrell

Roving from Nike to New Balance,
Prince to Puma, I pick up a pair
of size 13s, some shorts and blue sweats,
still feeling the sneakered beast scuff
his muzzle against my skull.

Two tall, hard-shouldered young brothaz
fondle *Air Jordans*, talkin' a little shit:
If I getchu down on the block
*wit **deez**   muhfuckas'll be callin' you* **Betty**.

"A drowning man," Mooji wrote, "is not
interested in air"   and as the few stars
that pardoned my life burn down, I recognize
this snag in my chest, this cut breath, this

lonely, late mid-life knowing: the inescapable
all around me, desperation all around—my own

stumbly efforts at love, my own
trying to say   *say something,*
while the duck-speaking dickheads
salute their zombie platoons.

Always big, bad Death posting me up,
backing me down, the ball's trick bounce
busting my brain: I know He's smooth
with either hand, but still mean
to snuff his shot.

                    In my college days,
when my parents were well
and the bulk of worry sat elsewhere,
I strolled around with *my boys* and mostly,
we wanted the same things:

to play sports, "make big bucks," and have
the fine babes find the come-hither in our faces.

What I miss   is that damn sure *hellyeah!*
we carried like crisp cash. JC, his wit,
that manic laugh—Eric's slick grin
and Doc, so thin only his head
cast shadow: that loud halo
of hair. "Don't touch the 'fro," he'd say.

I miss my boys and *The Ohio Players*
funkin' us up against the Earth's black hips—

> *...you a bad, bad missez*
> *with those skin-tight britches*
> *runnin' folks into ditches, yeah...*

We couldn't help ourselves.

There's a girl: a young woman, I guess
in her mid-20s, testing the exercise machines—
a serious athlete wearing sneaks that mean
speed, her righteous gluteous maximus rippling
each lift and pull. What I wish, now that I'm
older, is that she see through the three decades
between us   and work *my* back, but these days

I'm a *sir* a gray beard to be addressed
with deference, someone whose wisdom could
maybe be vaguely revered.

O Sex, song book of our better angels, how I craved
and savored your generous pages—chapter
and verse   and verse: kissing for hours, daylight lost
to the liquid velvet of the tongue, the body:
delicious synagogue, cello hungry to be bowed.

I don't believe the longing ever ends. I can't believe
I'll ever understand what I need to understand,

but in college I told Doc, "Prob'ly by the time
I'm forty   things won't get to me as much."

As I look at my life, I'm afraid   and earlier today,
in the mirror, I saw my mother's face
shocked at how old I am. *My goodness! How old
are you?*
                    And when I tell her, she's sure
I'm lying—and to be honest, I just
don't know if I'm the age I am. Each year
part of a conversation   I almost had
with someone I meant to call.

You think maybe all you do adds up
to a definable sum: the eulogy,
a small fire that lets survivors
warm their chilly hands, but really
nobody knows
what turned inside you or why
evolution has guaranteed that
none of us stick around. Last night,

a friend shrugged, "Might as well be positive,"
and I want to believe in people   because I'm a person:

I think about kindness, how it flickers
in a darkened place

and lynching—how some people loved it—
and Malcolm X, his soul sweetened after Mecca,

dying with buckshot scalding his chest,
but who ever mentions Yuri Kochiyama

holding his head in her lap. I believe
in the last light of her hand on his cheek.

Across the street, beneath a sky-blue sky, trees
black-barked and bare. I'm in a café now, surrounded
by clattery laughs and scrambled chatter, a mad jazz
that would scatter birds. What is it
with this world? A while back,

one of my boys died. I heard about it long after—
the funeral, somewhere in Georgia—so in my mind's eye,
Dewey's still *doin' the bump*, party-whistle gleaming
in his mouth, "Jungle Boogie" forever *rockin' the house*.

I used to think my lucky days made me
different somehow— "some angel
payin' my way"—like my mom said,
but this poem

could just as easily be Dewey, almost
remembering me   at the same party,

under the same groove: my fantastic history
filed down to a few finger-pops and some *Kool*

and The Gang. It's hard to breathe
without the delusion that magnified my life.

I sat across from him in class. We both
wrote poetry. Does everyone secretly

believe they're indispensable? I sit
inside this self   amazed by my face

which is brown and unremarkable.

THE HILT

Third Session

My sandbox, I remember—and
the morning glories my brother
planted and my mother dancing the
jitterbug in the living room with my
father shaking peanuts in his fist.

Even when she smiles, you see the past
disappearing in her eyes

He used to love the Les McCann trio,
that mad sax, the way he'd holler

Tryin' ta make it real…
like he was in the band.

Like creatures that suddenly find bars around them, I think they're
afraid, though my father laughs about "going to seed" and my mother
still brightens when the phone rings. I don't really know what's

happening inside my parents. It's like watching them through thick
glass.

Some days I think
I have never
known them:

they were
good at not
showing
all they felt.

The time
they lived in
required this.

In the parking lot: a starling, under cars then out, finally finds a French fry. I think of my life—moment to moment, move into move—my mind selling me its triggers and doubts.

Memory like a hammer   like a rope binding your wrists. Each step hobbled by this or that. Still: the feet float—

one in front of the other—

Consciousness: door through which
it all comes   as air walks
into a wound   as light

makes the movie in my head—
see this   now this.

Away from the city,
you can see all the stars
shed across the dark

and with the distance,
you're actually looking
back centuries, but

how ever you are, you
remain on Earth. Forget
the stars. Look down:

the customs of insects
are older than
all of us—

a fly rubs
its forelegs together
almost in prayer;

two ants
touch antennae,
why?— Think

of all
you've missed

re-thinking these hours
into something

you can say:

Another day, the man
in the parking lot shouting:

"You know
what *IT* wants!" he says,
"You know."

I try not to

see him:
no place to live, nobody
listening—

nobody listening—

my scone half-
eaten, coffee shop
music like gnats.

It wants to make you a thing in a story, a dumb thing,

a poor thing, a thing "of color", a go-along thing,

a get-a-job thing, a "white" thing   in a story

about things in a story about angry things

with things to do. Right now, the thing

is writing things down, plotting things out—

It is disguised as   just the way things are

There is a self you were
that you would be again, a place
you could return to. Not nostalgia:

say, you find yourself

drowning   and your eyes
show you only miles of water, you
still remember the shore.

Bonanza   Gun Smoke   The Rifleman

My father stares at the television   like he wishes he were *inside*.

Fear risen
like a new constellation—

    the sky beneath my skin.
Watching my parents

    begin to die. *Is this*
the grown-up you

    thought you'd be? Each minute
over-filling my hands, the hours

    spilled farther and farther
behind. Someone has to remember.

    No. Someone is working
a machine   whose controls

    you don't understand

My father cutting the hedges,
    I remember   and that sound
        a crayon makes in a coloring

        book—school days, my
          mother tickling us awake, I
            remember, and the way a

            cricket walks beneath
              a tree, the time it takes
                to get inside the grass.

Ape   in a cage —

does any other animal go insane?

Have you been here again? Smell of coffee.
      Some people sitting.
      Your table clear but for crumbs
      and some scratches.

    Some music with static, some sugar—
      those small brown packs.

      Outside in the parking lot,
        is that you?

THIRTY-THIRTY BLUES VILLANELLE

Who can tell a man not to go where he goes?
I laid the long tracks; my life waves from the train
I was thirty almost thirty years ago

Being grown up means you're s'posed to know,
Although *I don't know* what I can explain—
And I was thirty, like thirty years ago

I bend with the music breaking hard but slow
Jobs kidnap the daylight, then leave the remains:
"Just kiss me goodbye   when it's time to go"

It looks like we're losin' but say it ain't so:
Dumb news and new killers get most'a the fame
Why tell a man not to run when he goes?

My Dad's on a walker, his whole life in tow
If you'd seen him at forty you'd say *what a shame*,
But he was forty almost fifty years ago

Sanity pretends to pretend that you know
You've seen some good friends go off in the brain
Luck's hand was better than their hands could show

Why needle a riddle when the answer is no?
Been poking the troubles, but the Trouble remains
And I've been thirty since thirty years ago

I look at young men and think *where did I go?*
Play some guitar while Death tunes my name

Guess this is the *what*   I should already know
'Cause I was thirty thirty years ago

CHAPTER 6

MOSAIC

A carpet of light, the
ocean alive < half a moon
muting the stars.

I tell myself
despair   is just

a bad attitude: *Get up,*
I say. *Look—*
and the shimmer

spends its name
in my head.

_____

These days   mid-life
holds the jagged edge:

my nephew in prison,
a *prisoner* > friends insane

with work or sick
of trying to be loved,

my parents handing over their lives
like evidence: my good mother,

her mind   a trail of crumbs
in a woods flocked with birds.

          --/--

To *raise* a child   break it
like a wild horse—

bend the will: *get up,*
get dressed.

I remember Emlen School
staring me down, my lunch box,
September:
the spiked fence freshly painted.

Then, the goodbye from my mother
who'd fought my hard hair,
lipstick like mist on my cheek.

     --/--

That instant when eyes meet
and slide away—even love
blinks, looks off

like a stranger.

With: Who are you
with?

     --/--

I suspect   *everything.*

Outside the air moves
a giant bird I cannot see.

Still laced in this
brown body: my aging heart—
kah doom   kah doom-doom—
still minds my thoughts,

but rolls his eyes.

———

To see > < to be seen: the life
of the visible. *Don't be shy.*

Glances pick my face.

Once, I was a sperm and an egg,
but you didn't see me.

--/--

Too small to walk
alone: I held
my father's index
finger. Philadelphia police

caped in their black
jackets— big badges   almost

hungry— looking at us.

--/--

In a mall: say a *food court*
on Saturday   or a stadium
just before the game.

There's this drone, this
steady, muttering thrum

punctured by
packages—plastic this,
paper that—torn and torn.

"It's hard not to be hungry."

--/--

Time   for bed: my
mother reading *The
Three Little Pigs*, doing
all the voices. Remember
the pictures—those piggy
pants and shirts?

--/--

When you   *see me*,
what is that

image in the eye?
Solid ghosts, we are pictured
here—in the lit world.

Visible: we *want* to be seen: skin,
fancy legs   shoes and hats.

To want > to be seen and
wanted. Nice lips with a moist

sheen. Eyes, like mouths.

———

What tortures, what tortures
me   is the question: *what*
are other people   thinking?

I keep watch—a vast horde
of *Nikes* has landed, running
sea   to shining sea.

                --/--

In America skin was
where you belonged, a who

you were   *with*, a reason

someone might: how—*at the*

parties   of hands unknown—

astonishing deaths
could meet you.

———

Reckless eyeballs.

Three centuries track me,
their dumb dogs slobbering
on my scent: Myself runs

into my   other self: *Over here!*

my self whispers—*Freedom*

over here!

           --/--

Six-years-old, I sang
like a chickadee. My father

slapped me for handing him
the scissors

wrong. What did I know?
What did I know?

           --/--

Suppose nobody knows
what's
inside you.
But you, yourself,
find it pretty clear:

anxiety   adding up, leveling off,
doubling > some comfort in people
you think you
understand / frustration,

fatigue, a secret.
One worn constellation
marking the lusciousness of sex.

           --/--

What's your faith? Which skin
do you believe? The *unseen*

stays with us:
the air

rubbing your lungs
right now—

nations of germs
feuding over your hands.

        --/--

Savory sweet salt of sweat in summer,
a taste of almonds, some buttery bread.

The loins, a house of hunger, personal
but not personal: the way moonlight calls

for you and   not for you. What
I want >   I guess   < *I want.*

Fingernails grow. My
belly grumbles. My blood runs

up a long hill.

—————

Among *the brothaz*, a certain
grip   in the eyes. A sense

of something
swallowed   not chewed—

as if they'd been made
a story and were dying

to untell themselves:
profiles—prisons,

the sports inside The Sport.
Outside, the wolf

with a
huff   and a puff.

                --/--

Culture: a kind of knife:
cuts one way   opens
your brain to a certain
breed of light   shaves
consciousness to its

purpose, its cross: the nail
thru your hand > < your
other hand holding
the hammer.

                --/--

Once, I asked my father
if he knew   *everything*.

I was hopeful, seven—
a corn muffin
where my head shoulda been.

I saw him shave and after,
little dabs of Kleenex on the nicks.

                --/--

I only see
The Game   in pieces—
the rules inside me
like bad wiring < like a shadow
government < like dark
matter in a sky
otherwise Mardi Grased

with stars. Rise up,
somebody   somebody

       --/--

(Insert your life here.)

       --/--

Did you mean to be this way?
Did you mean to become
something you didn't mean?

*You didn' become
something you   didn'
mean   did you?*

       --/--

Image follows image, quack follows
quack— a line of lonely ducks. What

is wrong   is well

organized: see all the schedules
with their *Coors Lights* and comfy socks.

———

How do I look? With whom > < am I with?

Better worlds build hives
inside us. Last words

trapped like wasps in our mouths.

       --/--

So monogamy   never made
sense to me, nor most of what
was called *growing up.*

The whole
haunted house

of race and religion   of sex,
money   possession:

am I rented or owned?
How many lives turned
on the spit? How many
hours _____
and _____?

      --/--

I was nine, integrating Anna
Blakiston Day School: fourth grade,

mixing it up. Visible,

with my new face.
Whenever my mother
had to go see the teachers,

she'd say,
"Don't send me into battle

with a butter knife."

      --/--

Connect this to that, *this*
to that: word   by word, a
sentence

scavenges the alleys
like a lost pet—fur matted,
leg cut: the hunger,

a sort of riddle > his noise
some sort of answer.

————

What skinny faith you have—
and such big teeth: *all*

the better. I mean to step out
of history   for just a minute,

to feel my blood float

above the *say-so*. Memory,
a jar of flies. Spin off the lid.

I forget what you know. What

did you ever know?

                --/--

To speak: score the alphabet—
make the shape of what

cannot be seen. Tear it open

like a child with a new bag
of something / stand in the traffic

goading your throat until the song
sharpens in your mouth—

the solo: one nick

chasing another.

                --/--

I think I'm
starting to know
Everything < O, tongue!
O, summer! O, bold,
bare legs of women
upon which my soul beads
like sweat > O, rosemary rolls
and marmalade!

Hard-bodied beetles
with your six-legged sashay!
O,
funky beats and bitter
guitars < O, children
taller and taller no
matter
what!

O, moonlit sea! O, Hershey bars!
O, bizness be-suited
pigeons of death: *How   much
does   it   cost?*

———

One dandelion head gone to seed,
half-flung on the wind.

I've sold a lot of myself already:
already alotta my selves been sold.

I have this feeling

every day—*something* I know
that can't

be words. This life

stuffs my eyes.

These people nearby—syllables

like pheasants flushed
from their mouths.

I'm back on my mother's lap
waving my small arms.

1944

1949

1949

1967

1958

1960

END NOTES

Page 14: "The sugar cannot taste itself," was said by Ritodgata Myrti.

Page 44–45: "Death hides in the world / so we disguise ourselves" are lines from Erica Funkhouser's poem "Tae Kwon Do." (found in her collection, *Sure Shot*)

Page 68: The entirety of Mooji's quote: "A starving man is not interested in food, nor is a drowning man interested in air. For one longing for Liberation, self-knowledge is not an interest, it is vital."

The phrase "posting me up" refers to playing basketball closer to the basket—"on the block," the rectangle painted from baseline to foul line, usually the domain of the bigger players.

Page 85: Florence Church is credited with the epigraph. She was my great grandmother on my mother's side.

Page 86: "...*kah doom kah doom-doom*": sounds from Etheridge Knight's poem "Ilu, The Talking Drum." (found in *The Essential Etheridge Knight*)

Books from Etruscan Press

Zarathustra Must Die | Dorian Alexander
The Disappearance of Seth | Kazim Ali
Drift Ice | Jennifer Atkinson
Crow Man | Tom Bailey
Coronology | Claire Bateman
What We Ask of Flesh | Remica L. Bingham
The Greatest Jewish-American Lover in Hungarian History | Michael Blumenthal
No Hurry | Michael Blumenthal
Choir of the Wells | Bruce Bond
Cinder | Bruce Bond
The Other Sky | Bruce Bond and Aron Wiesenfeld
Peal | Bruce Bond
Poems and Their Making: A Conversation | Moderated by Philip Brady
Crave: Sojourn of a Hungry Soul | Laurie Jean Cannady
Toucans in the Arctic | Scott Coffel
Body of a Dancer | Renée E. D'Aoust
Scything Grace | Sean Thomas Dougherty
Surrendering Oz | Bonnie Friedman
Nahoonkara | Peter Grandbois
The Candle: Poems of Our 20th Century Holocausts | William Heyen
The Confessions of Doc Williams & Other Poems | William Heyen
The Football Corporations | William Heyen
A Poetics of Hiroshima | William Heyen
Shoah Train | William Heyen
September 11, 2001: American Writers Respond | Edited by William Heyen
American Anger: An Evidentiary | H. L. Hix
As Easy As Lying | H. L. Hix
As Much As, If Not More Than | H. L. Hix
Chromatic | H. L. Hix
First Fire, Then Birds | H. L. Hix
God Bless | H. L. Hix
I'm Here to Learn to Dream in Your Language | H. L. Hix
Incident Light | H. L. Hix

Etruscan Press is Proud of Support Received from

Wilkes University

Youngstown State University

The Ohio Arts Council

The Stephen & Jeryl Oristaglio Foundation

The Nathalie & James Andrews Foundation

The National Endowment for the Arts

The Ruth H. Beecher Foundation

The Bates-Manzano Fund

The New Mexico Community Foundation

Drs. Barbara Brothers & Gratia Murphy Fund

The Rayen Foundation

The Pella Corporation

The Raymond John Wean Foundation

Founded in 2001 with a generous grant from the Oristaglio Foundation, Etruscan Press is a nonprofit cooperative of poets and writers working to produce and promote books that nurture the dialogue among genres, achieve a distinctive voice, and reshape the literary and cultural histories of which we are a part.

etruscan press

www.etruscanpress.org

Etruscan Press books may be ordered from

Consortium Book Sales and Distribution
800.283.3572
www.cbsd.com

Etruscan Press is a 501(c)(3) nonprofit organization.
Contributions to Etruscan Press are tax deductible
as allowed under applicable law.
For more information, a prospectus,
or to order one of our titles,
contact us at books@etruscanpress.org.